T0197372

EVERY DAY I AM

Written By:
Alyson E. Calloway

Inspired By:
Thomas D. Edwards III

Illustrated By:
AB Digital Designing

© 2020 Alyson Calloway. All rights reserved.

No part of this book may be reproduced, stored in a retrieval system, or
transmitted by any means without the written permission of the author.

AuthorHouse™
1663 Liberty Drive
Bloomington, IN 47403
www.authorhouse.com
Phone: 1 (833) 262-8899

Because of the dynamic nature of the Internet, any web addresses or links contained
in this book may have changed since publication and may no longer be valid. The views
expressed in this work are solely those of the author and do not necessarily reflect the
views of the publisher, and the publisher hereby disclaims any responsibility for them.

Any people depicted in stock imagery provided by Getty Images are models,
and such images are being used for illustrative purposes only.
Certain stock imagery © Getty Images.

This book is printed on acid-free paper.

ISBN: 978-1-7283-7214-3 (sc)
      978-1-7283-7215-0 (hc)
      978-1-7283-7213-6 (e)

Library of Congress Control Number: 2020916511

Print information available on the last page.

Published by AuthorHouse 09/02/2020

For every boy and girl that dares to live life believing that anything is possible for them. The world is waiting for you!

To my why, may you always realize the limitless power that resides within you. You are loved. You are special. You, my son, are going to change this world. Just you wait!

Every day, before I go to school,
Mommy lets me say words that
are very cool.

I am STRONG!

They help me to focus and make
me so proud.
Sometimes I like to say them
really, really loud.

I am MIGHTY!

She always tells me that there
isn't anything I can't do.
And that God protects and guides
me, too.

I am BRILLIANT!

I can use my big brain, I can use my great mind to think powerful things about myself all of the time.

I am BEAUTIFUL!

When the day is over and I go to
sleep at night,
Mommy tells me how amazing I
am and I know that she is right.

Jesus loves ME!

I am

I look forward to waking up and going to see my friends, because I get to say cool words all over again.

I can do ANYTHING!

Repeat after me:
I am STRONG!
I am MIGHTY!
I am BRILLIANT
I am BEAUTIFUL!
Jesus loves ME!
AND...
I can do ANYTHING!

I am
STRONG

I am
MIGHTY

I am
BRILLIANT

I CAN DO ANYTHING

I am BEAUTIFUL

JESUS LOVES ME

Printed in the United States
By Bookmasters